The Lucky Cookbook

Let the Luck of the Irish Rule Your Kitchen

Table of Contents

Introduction

Ireland has never been a rich country. However, agriculturally, it has an abundance of wealth. Vegetables grow easily in its fertile soil. Cows and lambs feed naturally on fresh grass for an unbeatable flavor. Irish butter is as rich and creamy as it gets. The recipes in this Lucky Irish Cookbook are genuinely created with superb ingredients.

It's a simple country, and the simplicity is reflected in its cooking. Since Ireland spent a lot of time under British rule, it has considerable English influence. It is also the reason why most dishes contain potatoes and cabbage. Everyone knows about the Great Irish Potato Famine. But this crisis was due less to a lack of potatoes than the fact that the English overlords demanded their share of every crop grown. This left the Irish with little to eat. They grew potatoes and cabbage because these vegetables were easy and cheap to grow. They learned to use potatoes and cabbage in a great many recipes.

Ireland loves its meat pies, and you'll find a few of these delectable recipes in this Lucky Irish Cookbook. The reason for these pies is that it was easy for miners, farmers, and other laborers to bring for lunch. Leftovers were cooked in a delicious crust and tucked in a pocket till lunchtime. This made it possible for miners, who spent 12 hours underground in darkness, to eat.

The Irish also love their Guinness. Many of the wonderful recipes in this book are flavored by the addition of some dark stout.

Hoist a pint and sing a happy Irish tune. Release your inner Irish with the recipes in the Lucky Irish Cookbook.

Breakfast

Full Irish Breakfast

This is a hearty breakfast with lots of meats that will fill you for a few hours. Grill soda bread (see recipe) to serve along with the rest. NOTE: Some people may have a problem with black pudding. If you don't feel like trying it (it's extremely tasty), substitute ham instead.

Cooking Time: 50 minutes

Servings: 2

Ingredients:

- 1 tbsp. olive oil
- 2 sliced tomatoes

- 2 cups cooked and cubed potatoes
- 6 thick slices bacon
- 4 breakfast sausages
- 4 oz. sliced black pudding
- 1 tbsp. butter
- 4 eggs
- 2 slices prepared soda bread

Directions:

1. Preheat the oven to 200 degrees.

2. Fry the bacon in a skillet until done, about 10 minutes.

3. Keep some of the bacon grease.

4. Place the bacon on a baking sheet and keep warm in oven.

5. Fry the breakfast sausage and black pudding for 5 minutes and keep warm in the oven.

6. Fry the potatoes for 10 minutes until they are crispy. Transfer to the oven to keep warm.

7. Fry the tomato slices in the skillet for 5 minutes, then place in oven to keep warm.

8. If you are out of bacon grease, heat 1 tbsp. of butter.

9. Fry the eggs sunny side up, about 5 minutes.

10. Transfer the eggs to 2 plates.

11. Fry the sliced soda bread for 5 minutes.

12. Spread the soda bread with some orange marmalade.

13. Add the tomatoes, potatoes, bacon, sausage, black pudding and soda bread to each plate.

Treacle Scones

Serve with some butter and jam for a tasty breakfast. These scones aren't overly sweet, so they can be enjoyed anytime. They can also serve as a biscuit along with a meal.

Cooking Time: 12 minutes

Servings: 14

Ingredients:

- 4 cups flour
- 2 ½ tsp. baking soda
- 2 tsp. lemon juice
- ½ tsp. salt
- 1 tsp. allspice

- ½ tsp. cinnamon
- ¾ cup butter
- 3 tbsp. molasses
- 1 tbsp. sugar
- 1 cup buttermilk

Directions:

1. Preheat the oven to 425 degrees.

2. Coat a baking sheet with non-stick spray.

3. Combine the flour, baking soda, lemon juice, salt, allspice and cinnamon in a bowl.

4. Stir the molasses, sugar and buttermilk together.

5. Add the buttermilk to the flour and stir just enough to combine.

6. Flour a flat surface and lightly knead the dough.

7. Roll the dough out and create ½ thick rounds

8. Bake for 12 minutes.

9. Let cool before eating.

Irish Soda Bread

Nice and crusty and just a bit sweet. Serve as toast or with meals.

Cooking Time: 45 minutes

Servings: 18

Ingredients:

- 4 cups flour
- ¼ cup sugar
- ½ tsp. salt
- ½ cup butter
- 2 cups milk
- 1 tsp. baking soda
- 2 tbsp. vinegar
- 1 cup raisins
- 1 tbsp. baking powder

Directions:

1. Preheat the oven to 375 degrees.

2. Coat a baking sheet with non-stick spray

3. Combine the sugar, baking soda, flour, baking powder, salt and butter.

4. Add the milk and vinegar and stir.

5. Fold in the raisins.

6. Create a dough ball and place it on the baking sheet.

7. Bake for 45 minutes.

Corned Beef Hash

You can make corned beef especially for the hash or use any leftover corned beef you have. Top the hash with fried or poached eggs.

Cooking Time: 20 minutes

Servings: 8

Ingredients:

- 3 tbsp. butter
- 1 chopped onion
- 5 peeled and cubed potatoes

- 1 chopped red pepper
- 1 tbsp. chopped parsley
- ½ tsp. thyme
- ¼ tsp. rosemary
- Salt and peppers to taste
- ¼ tsp. oregano
- 2 lb. cubed corned beef

Directions:

1. Melt the butter in a skillet

2. Sauté the onion for 5 minutes.

3. Stir in the potatoes and red pepper and cook for 15 minutes.

4. Season the potatoes with the parsley, herbs, salt and pepper.

5. Add the corned beef and cook for another 10 minutes.

Appetizers

Cheesy Cookies

Great appetizer with a nice glass of wine. They have a delicious smoky flavor.

Cooking Time: 10 minutes

Servings: 40

Ingredients:

- 1 stick of butter, cut into small pieces
- 6 oz. shredded sharp cheddar cheese
- ½ tsp. salt
- ½ tsp. chipotle powder

- 1 ½ cups flour

Directions:

1. Place the butter, cheese, salt and chipotle powder in a food processor and process until you get a grainy consistency.

2. Add the flour and continue to process.

3. Transfer the dough to a flat surface and knead for a few minutes.

4. Create small balls and place them on a baking sheet lined with parchment paper.

5. Press down on the balls with a fork. The thinner the cookie, the crispier it will be.

6. Freeze the dough for 2 hours.

7. Preheat the oven to 350 degrees.

8. Bake cookies for 10 minutes.

Beer Cheese Dip

Find a soccer game and lay out a bowl of pretzels and some soda bread and this tip. You'll feel as Irish as Saint Patrick.

Cooking Time: 30 minutes

Servings: 16

Ingredients:

- 2 cups diced smoked gouda
- 2 cups diced Dubliner cheese
- 1 cup stout beer
- 1 tbsp. Worcestershire sauce

- ½ tsp. garlic powder

Directions:

1. Add the ingredients to a pan and cook on low until everything is melted and combined. This can take 30 minutes while you keep stirring.

Main Meals

Sausage Coddle

A traditional stew with a great creamy sauce.

Cooking Time: 1 hour 40 minutes

Servings: 8

Ingredients:

- 1 lb. sausage
- ½ lb. cubed bacon
- 2 sliced onions
- 3 peeled and sliced potatoes

- 2 diced parsnip

- 2 cups sliced mushrooms

- Salt and pepper to taste

- 2 cups beef stock

- ¾ cup Guinness

- 1/3 cup half and half

Directions:

1. Preheat the oven to 325 degrees.

2. Add the sausages and bacon to a skillet and cook for 10 minutes.

3. Slice the sausages and set aside with the bacon

4. In a 9x13 baking dish, create 3 layers of potatoes, parsnips, mushrooms, sausage, and bacon.

5. Season with salt and pepper.

6. Pour the Guinness and half and half into the baking dish.

7. Bake for 1 ½ hours.

Bangers and Mash

An inexpensive dinner that can be made with any good sausage or bratwurst.

Cooking Time: 45 minutes

Servings: 4

Ingredients:

- 2 lb. peeled and cubed potatoes
- 5 tbsp. butter
- Salt and pepper to taste

- 4 large sausages
- 2 chopped onions
- 1 bottle dark beer
- 2 tbsp. butter
- 2 cups beef broth
- ½ cup red wine
- 1 tsp. Worcestershire sauce

Directions:

1. Boil the potatoes in a pot of salted water for 15 minutes until done.

2. Mash the potatoes with a fork and stir in the butter.

3. Season with salt and pepper and keep warm.

4. Fry the sausages and onions for 10 minutes.

5. Add the beer and cook for another 10 minutes until the beer is reduced.

6. Stir in the butter and add the broth, wine and Worcestershire sauce.

7. Cook on high until the broth is reduced to a desired consistency, around 10 minutes.

8. Divide the sausages and mashed potato on plates and top with the gravy.

Stuffed Leg of Lamb

This lamb is teeming with flavors. Serve with roasted potatoes.

Cooking Time: 51 minutes

Servings: 8

Ingredients:

- 5-lb. boneless leg of lamb
- Salt and black pepper to taste
- 1 tsp. Montreal Steak Spice
- 1 tbsp. olive oil

- 2 minced garlic cloves
- 1 bag of baby spinach
- 1 cup goat cheese
- ¼ tsp. rosemary
- ½ cup flour
- Salt and pepper as needed.
- 1 tsp rosemary
- 1 tbsp. olive oil

Directions:

1. Place the leg of lamb on a cutting board.

2. Use a mallet to pound the lamb to less than an inch thickness.

3. Preheat the oven to 400 degrees.

4. Season the lamb with salt, pepper and Montreal Steak Spice.

5. Heat the olive oil and sauté the garlic for 5 minutes.

6. Season the garlic with rosemary.

7. Add the spinach and cook for 1 minute.

8. Crumble the cheese and combine with the sautéed garlic.

9. Cover the leg of lamb with the spinach.

10. Spread the flavored cheese across the leg of lamb.

11. Roll up the leg of lamb and tie with a string.

12. Combine the salt, pepper and rosemary and stir into the flour.

13. Coat the leg of lamb with the flour.

14. Heat the olive oil in a cast-iron skillet.

15. Brown the leg on all sides for 5 minutes.

16. Place the skillet in the oven – 40 minutes for medium doneness.

17. Let the leg of lamb rest for 10 minutes before slicing.

Braised Lamb Shanks

These are really juicy and tender.

Cooking Time: 2 hours 30 minutes

Servings: 4

Ingredients:

- 2 tbsp. olive oil
- ¼ cup flour
- 4 lamb shanks
- 1 chopped onion
- 3 minced garlic cloves
- 1 bottle stout

- 1 ¾ cups beef broth
- Salt and pepper to taste
- 1 tsp. brown sugar
- 4 fresh thyme sprigs
- 2 fresh rosemary sprigs
- 1 bay leaf
- 3 peeled and chopped carrots
- 2 peeled and cubed potatoes
- 2 cubed parsnip

Directions:

1. Heat the olive oil in a Dutch oven.

2. Place the lamb shanks and flour in a plastic bag and shake to coat the meat.

3. Brown the lamb shanks for 10 minutes.

4. Transfer the lamb shanks to a platter.

5. Add the onion and garlic to the Dutch oven and sauté for 5 minutes.

6. Pour in the beer and broth.

7. Season with salt and pepper.

8. Stir in the brown sugar

9. Place the lamb shanks back in the Dutch oven.

10. Create a bouquet garni by putting the herbs in a cheesecloth and tying with a piece of string.

11. Add the bouquet garni to the Dutch oven.

12. Simmer for 1 ½ hours.

13. Stir in the carrots, potatoes and parsnip and simmer for 45 minutes, until the vegetables are done.

14. Discard the bouquet garni

Irish Lamb Stew

This stew definitely tastes better the second day – if you can wait that long.

Cooking Time: 8 hours 5 minutes

Servings: 8

Ingredients:

- ½ lb. diced bacon
- 5 lb. cubed lamb meat
- Salt and pepper to taste
- 3 minced garlic cloves
- 1 chopped onion

- 3 chopped celery sticks
- 3 cups beef stock
- 3 peeled and sliced carrot
- 3 cubed potatoes
- 1 tsp. rosemary
- 2 bay leaves
- 2 cups stout beer
- ¼ cup cornstarch

Directions:

1. Fry the bacon in a skillet until crispy.

2. Retain a tablespoon of bacon fat in the skillet and sauté the garlic and onion for 5 minutes.

3. Drain the bacon on a paper towel and crumble.

4. Place all ingredients in a slow cooper and stir well.

5. Cook on low for 7 hours.

6. Ladle out 1 cup of broth and combine with the cornstarch.

7. Pour the cornstarch into the slow cooker.

8. Cook for 1 more hour.

Corned Beef and Cabbage

Think of those yummy sandwiches …. Interestingly, corned beef is an addition brought to the New World by Irish immigrants. In Ireland, poor farmers couldn't afford corned beef, so their St. Patrick's Day dish was actually boiled bacon and cabbage. We think the corned beef is a change for the better.

Cooking Time: 4 hours 10 minutes

Servings: 8

Ingredients:

- 4-lb. corned beef with spice packet
- 2 tsp. Dijon mustard
- 8 cups of chicken broth
- 2 cups of dark ale
- 2 quartered onions
- 3 chunked carrots
- 1 cubed parsnip
- Salt and pepper to taste
- ½ tsp. thyme
- 1 ½ lb. peeled and halved small potatoes
- 1 cabbage cut into 8 chunks.

Directions:

1. Coat the corned beef with mustard

2. Sprinkle with the contents of the spice packet.

3. Place the corned beef in a Dutch oven.

4. Pour the broth and ale over the corned beef.

5. Add the onion and season with salt, pepper and thyme.

6. Simmer for 3 hours.

7. Add the potatoes, parsnip and carrots.

8. Cook for another 30 minutes. The vegetables should be almost tender.

9. Add the cabbage and cook for 20 minutes.

10. Transfer the corned beef to a cutting board and let sit for 20 minutes.

11. Slice across the grain.

12. Serve the slices with vegetables and broth.

Irish Steaks

Enjoy some delicious grass-fed beef.

Cooking Time: 21 minutes

Servings: 4

Ingredients:

- ¼ cup butter
- 2 chopped onions
- 2 cups sliced mushrooms
- 2 minced garlic cloves
- 4 steaks of your choice
- Salt and pepper to taste

- ¼ cup Irish whiskey
- Salt and ground black pepper to taste

Directions:

1. Heat the butter in a large skillet.

2. Sauté the onions and mushrooms for 8 minutes.

3. Stir in the garlic and sauté for 2 more minutes.

4. Remove the vegetables to a platter.

5. Add the steaks and cook 4 minutes each side for medium.

6. Transfer the steaks to a platter.

7. Take the skillet from the stove and pour in the whiskey.

8. Stir the onion/mushroom mixture into the whiskey and simmer for 5 minutes.

9. Top the steaks with the onion/mushrooms.

10. Drizzle with any remaining sauce.

Chicken and Leek Pie

This resembles a chicken pot pie. It's easy and delicious. The egg is added to the broth for some extra thickness.

Cooking Time: 6

Servings: 6

Ingredients:

- 1 9-inch pastry crust
- 3 tbsp. butter
- 3 chopped leeks
- 1 chopped onion

- 2 tbsp. flour
- 3 ½ lb. chicken cut into small pieces
- 1 cup peas
- salt and pepper to taste
- ½ tsp. sage
- ½ tsp. thyme
- 1 cup chicken stock
- 1 beaten egg
- 1/3 cup heavy cream

Directions:

1. Preheat the oven to 350 degrees.

2. Create several layers of chicken and onions in a baking dish

3. Season the layers with salt, pepper, sage, and thyme.

4. Whip the egg and broth together

5. Pour the broth and heavy cream over the chicken

6. Bake for 55 minutes.

Potato Leek Soup

The French would love to take credit for Potato Leek Soup. Mais, non. The Irish came first, when they needed a way to stretch those precious potatoes. They serve their "tattie and leekie" hot. For an awesome presentation, serve the soup in sourdough bread bowls.

Cooking Time: 35 minutes

Servings: 8

Ingredients:

- ½ cup butter

- 2 washed and sliced leeks
- Salt and pepper to taste
- 3 minced garlic cloves
- 4 cups chicken broth
- 4 cups peeled and diced potatoes
- 2 cups half and half
- Toppings: either ½ cup of shredded cheddar cheese or ¼ cup chopped dill

Directions:

1. Melt the butter in a soup pot.

2. Sauté the leeks for 10 minutes and season with salt and pepper.

3. Stir in the garlic and cook for 5 more minutes.

4. Pour the chicken broth over the leeks.

5. Stir in the potatoes and bring the broth to a boil.

6. Add the half and half and simmer for 20 minutes.

7. Use an immersion blender to create a smooth soup.

8. Top with shredded cheese or dill.

Irish Vegetable Soup

Ireland is great farm country and a great place for vegetable soup.

Cooking Time: 20 minutes

Servings: 6

Ingredients:

- 4 chopped carrots
- 2 peeled and cubed potatoes
- 1 peeled and diced parsnip
- 1 peeled and diced turnip

- 1 peeled and diced squash
- 1 chopped onion
- 4 cups vegetable broth
- Salt and pepper to taste
- ½ tsp. thyme
- ½ tsp. rosemary
- 1 bunch baby spinach
- ½ cup heavy cream

Directions:

1. Place all ingredients except the spinach and heavy cream in large pot.

2. Make sure there is enough broth to cover the vegetables.

3. Bring the broth to a boil and cook for 15 minutes, until the vegetables are tender.

4. Place half of the vegetable in a blender to puree.

5. Return the pureed vegetables to the pot and add the spinach and heavy cream.

6. Stir and cook for 5 more minutes.

Cabbage Soup

Wonderfully filling cabbage soup. Great in cold weather.

Cooking Time: 50 minutes

Servings: 4

Ingredients:

- 6 slices diced thick bacon
- 1 diced onion
- 2 cups peeled and cubed potatoes
- 15 oz. canned diced tomatoes with juice
- 2 cups chicken stock

- Salt and black pepper to taste
- 1 tsp. sugar
- ½ tsp. basil
- 2 cups shredded cabbage
- 1 ½ cup cooked shredded chicken

Directions:

1. Fry the bacon in a skillet for 10 minutes.

2. Drain on a paper towel.

3. Keep a tbsp. of bacon fat in the skillet and sauté the onion for 5 minutes.

4. Place all ingredients except the cabbage and chicken in a pot and simmer for 25 minutes.

5. Stir in the shredded chicken and cabbage and simmer for 10 minutes.

Cottage Pie

Great quick dinner, and an excellent way to use leftovers.

Cooking Time: 57 minutes

Servings: 4

Ingredients:

- 1 lb. ground beef
- 1 diced onion
- 3 peeled and diced carrots
- 1 cup thawed frozen peas
- 2 tbsp. flour

- ½ tsp. oregano
- ½ tsp. basil
- 1 ¼ cups beef broth
- 1 tbsp. ketchup
- ½ tsp Lee & Perrins
- Salt and pepper to taste
- 4 peeled and diced potatoes
- ½ tsp. thyme
- ¼ cup butter
- ¼ cup milk
- Salt and pepper to taste
- 1/3 lb. shredded Cheddar cheese

Directions:

Preheat oven to 400 degrees.

Sauté the beef in a skillet for 2 minutes.

Stir in the onion, carrots and peas and sauté for 5 more minutes.

Then add the flour and herbs and combine well.

Combine the broth and ketchup and add to the beef mixture.

Season with salt and butter.

Let the mixture simmer for 15 minutes.

Transfer the filling to a pie dish.

Cook the potatoes in salted water for 10 minutes until done.

Mash the potatoes and stir in the milk and butter.

Season with salt and pepper.

Spoon the potatoes over the beef.

Top with the shredded cheese.

Bake for 25 minutes.

Steak and Kidney Pie

This steak and kidney pie has an amazing gravy.

Cooking Time: 1 hour 15 minutes

Servings: 6

Ingredients:

- 1 lb. beef or veal kidney
- 2 lb. beef stew meat
- 2 tbsp. olive oil
- 2 chopped onions
- Salt and pepper to taste

- ½ tsp. thyme
- 1 bay leaf
- 3 cups beef broth
- ¾ cup red wine
- 4 cups diced potatoes
- ¼ cup flour
- 1 prepared pie crust
- 1 cup of sliced mushrooms
- 1 beaten egg

Directions:

Dice the kidney meat or have your butcher do it.

Heat the olive oil in a pot and sauté the kidney and beef for 5 minutes.

Stir in the onion and season with salt, pepper, and thyme.

Add the bay leaf and 1 ½ cup broth and the wine.

Simmer for 40 minutes.

Add the potatoes and mushrooms and then continue to simmer for 30 minutes.

Combine the flour with 1 ½ cups beef broth and add to the mixture.

Stir well to thicken the sauce.

Transfer the filling to a casserole dish.

Top with the pie crust.

Brush the beaten egg over the crust and slice a few vents into the crust.

Bake for 30 minutes at 425 degrees.

Fish and Chips

Always a classic. Serve the fish with some vinegar on the side. The potatoes are fried twice for extraordinary crispness.

Cooking Time: 4

Servings: 4

- 4 potatoes sliced into strips
- 1 ¼ cup flour
- 1 tsp. baking soda
- Salt and pepper to taste
- ½ tsp. Old Bay seasoning
- 1 cup dark beer

- 1 beaten egg
- 4 cups canola oil
- 2 lb. halibut fillets

Directions:

1. Place the potatoes in a bowl of water overnight.

2. Combine the flour, baking soda, salt, pepper, Old Bay seasoning in a bowl.

3. Add the beer and egg and combine to create a batter.

4. Refrigerate the batter for 1 hour.

5. Heat the oil in a fryer or large skillet until very hot.

6. Fry the potatoes for 5 minutes, then drain on a paper towel.

7. Coat the fish with the batter.

8. Fry the fish until brown, about 5 minutes.

9. Drain on paper towels.

10. Fry the potatoes again for 2 minutes for extra crispness.

11. Serve with a side of vinegar.

Side Dishes

Creamed Cabbage

A creamy side dish. Fill a pita pocket with this creamy cabbage and you have a wonderful sandwich.

Cooking Time: 25 minutes

Servings: 6

Ingredients:

- 6 slices bacon
- 1 diced onion
- ¼ cup butter
- 2 tbsp. milk

- 1 tbsp. flour
- Sal to taste
- ½ head of shredded cabbage
- 4 oz. sour cream
- ½ tsp. smoky paprika

Directions:

1. Fry the bacon in a skillet for 10 minutes.

2. Drain the bacon on a paper towel.

3. Combine the butter, milk, flour, and milk in the skillet with the remaining bacon drippings.

4. Add the cabbage and cook on low for 15 minutes.

5. Crumble the bacon and add the bacon, sour cream and paprika to the cabbage.

Potatoes O'Brien

These can be a breakfast potato or a regular side dish.

Cooking Time: 30 minutes

Servings: 8

Ingredients:

- 6 large quartered potatoes
- 3 tbsp. vegetable oil
- 1 diced green bell pepper
- 1 diced red bell pepper

- 1 diced onion
- ½ tsp. Lawry's Seasoning Salt
- ¼ tsp. paprika

Directions:

1. Cooked the potatoes in a pot of salted water for 10 minutes, until done.

2. Drain the potatoes, then slice them.

3. Heat the oil in a skillet.

4. Combine all ingredients well.

5. Fry the potatoes and peppers on low heat for 20 minutes. The potatoes should be crisp.

Fried Cabbage

An excellent side dish and a different way to enjoy cabbage.

Cooking Time: 40 minutes

Servings: 6

Ingredients:

- 3 tsp. butter
- 1 ¼ cup chicken broth
- 1 tsp. cider vinegar

- 1 chopped head of cabbage
- 2 peeled and grated carrots
- Salt and pepper to taste

Directions:

1. Melt the butter in a skillet and stir in the chicken broth and cider vinegar.

2. Stir in the cabbage and carrots and simmer for 40 minutes.

3. Season with salt and pepper.

Cheddar Onion Soda Bread

This soda bread has a totally different flavor than the one above. Instead of being sweet, the cheese and onion turn it into a savory delight. Wonderful as an accompaniment to an Irish meal.

Cooking Time: 30 minutes

Servings: 8

Ingredients:

- 4 cups flour
- 1 tsp. salt

- 2 tsp. baking powder
- ¾ cup cold butter
- 1 ¼ cups buttermilk
- 1 beaten egg
- 6 chopped scallions
- 1 tsp. baking soda
- 2/3 cup shredded Cheddar cheese

Directions:

1. Preheat the oven to 425 degrees.

2. Line a baking sheet with parchment paper.

3. Combine the flour, baking powder, salt and baking soda in a bowl.

4. Whisk the buttermilk and egg together.

5. Add in the butter, buttermilk, scallions and shredded cheese to create a dough.

6. Shape two dough balls and place on the baking sheet.

7. Flatten the balls until they are 2 inches thick.

8. Bake for 30 minutes.

Mint Sauce

You can't enjoy good Irish lamb without some excellent mint sauce.

Cooking Time: 2 minutes

Servings: 4

Ingredients:

- 1 ½ cups chopped fresh mint
- ¼ cup beef broth
- 1/3 cup red wine vinegar
- 3 tbsp. sugar

Directions:

1. Combine the ingredients in a saucepan.

2. Simmer for 2 minutes and stir until the sugar is dissolved.

3. Refrigerate for 2 hours.

4. If needed, season with a bit of salt.

Desserts

Tea Cake

Enjoy this simple but delicious cake with tea or coffee. Fabulous either way.

Cooking Time: 45 minutes

Servings: 10

- ½ cup butter
- 1 cup white sugar
- 2 eggs
- 1 tsp. vanilla extract
- 1 ½ cups flour
- 2 tsp. baking powder

- 1/8 tsp. salt
- 1 cup milk
- 3 tbsp. sour cream
- 2 cups frozen raspberries
- 1 tbsp. raspberry liqueur
- 3 tbsp. sugar

Directions:

1. Preheat the oven to 350 degrees.

2. Coat a 9-inch cake pan with non-stick spray.

3. Whip the butter and sugar until creamy

4. Add one egg at a time and keep whipping.

5. Stir in the vanilla extract.

6. In another bowl, combine the flour, baking powder and salt.

7. Add the flour to the butter/sugar mixture.

8. Stir in the milk and sour cream.

9. Transfer the batter to the cake pan.

10. Bake for 45 minutes.

11. Let cool.

12. While the cake is baking, combine raspberries, raspberry liquor, 1 cup water and sugar in a saucepan.

13. Stir and bring to boil.

14. Let cool.

15. Spoon the raspberry sauce over the cake.

St. Patrick's Day Cake

This is extremely rich. If you don't want to buy expensive Bailey's Irish Cream, you can substitute Irish Cream coffee creamer.

Cooking Time: 35 minutes

Servings: 16

Ingredients:

- 1 cup Guinness
- 1 cup butter

- 2/3 cup cocoa powder
- 2 eggs
- 2 cups flour
- 2 cups white sugar
- 1 tsp. baking soda
- 1 cup sour cream
- 1 tsp. salt

Frosting

- 1 ½ cups whipping cream
- 1 cup semisweet chocolate.
- ¼ cup Bailey Irish cream liqueur
- 3 tbsp. butter

Directions:

1. Preheat the oven to 350 degrees.

2. Line 2 cake pans with parchment paper.

3. Heat the beer and butter in a saucepan while stirring

4. Remove from heat and stir in the cocoa powder to create a smooth mixture. Let cool.

5. Whisk the eggs and sour cream in a bowl using a hand mixer.

6. Stir in the beer mixture and combine until smooth.

7. Combine the flour, sugar, baking soda and salt in a larger bowl.

8. Pour in the beer mixture and stir until combined.

9. Transfer the batter into the cake pans.

10. Bake for 30 minutes and let cool.

11. Combine the frosting ingredients in a pan and heat while stirring for 5 minutes.

12. Frost the top of both cakes.

13. Place both cakes on top of each other and frost the sides.

Irish Cream Chocolate Mousse

This is deliciously creamy and lighter than pudding. Use real whipping cream instead of the prepared kind.

Cooking Time: 5 minutes

Servings: 8

Ingredients:

- 8 oz. chopped dark chocolate
- 6 eggs yolks
- 6 egg whites
- 2 tbsp. Irish cream liqueur

- 2 tbsp. strong coffee
- 1 cup heavy cream
- 1 tbsp. sugar

Directions:

1. Melt the chocolate in a pan and let it cool.

2. Whisk the egg yolks in a bowl.

3. Gently stir in the liqueur and coffee.

4. Whisk the heavy cream and sugar with a beater.

5. Spoon half the whipped cream into the chocolate mixture.

6. Beat the egg whites until stiff.

7. Fold the egg white into the mouse.

8. Transfer the mousse into serving dishes and top with some whipped cream.

Shortbread Cookies

Serve with some good coffee. Sit back and relax.

Cooking Time: 20 minutes

Servings: 12

- 1 ½ sticks butter
- 2 cups flour
- 1 cup confectioners' sugar
- ¾ cup cornstarch
- ½ tsp. vanilla extract
- 1/8 tsp. salt
- 2 oz. semi-sweet chocolate

Directions:

1. Blend all ingredients in a bowl. You can use your hands.

2. Create 1-inch rounds

3. Place the cookies on a cookie sheet

4. Use a fork to flatten the cookies.

5. Bake at 300 degrees for 20 minutes

6. Melt the chocolate (microwave is fine) as the cookies are baking.

7. Drizzle the melted chocolate over the shortbread cookies.

Barmbrack

This is a traditional holiday fruitcake. Usually, it has items baked into the slices that are meant to foretell the future: a ring means the receiver will get married; a piece of cloth means the receiver will not get married that year. It's fun and delicious. The fruits are soaked in tea (and a bit of Irish whiskey) to plump them up.

Cooking Time: 12

Servings: 10

Ingredients:

- ¼ cup dried currants
- ¼ cup raisins
- ¼ cup dried and chopped apricots
- ¼ cup candied citrus rinds
- 1 ¼ cup cold Irish tea
- 3 tbsp. Irish whiskey
- 1 tsp. cinnamon
- 1 tsp. cloves
- 1 tsp. allspice
- ½ tsp. nutmeg
- ½ tsp. baking soda
- 1 egg
- 1 ½ cups sugar
- 1 ¾ cups flour

Directions:

1. Soak the fruits in tea/whiskey for 2 hours.

2. Drain the liquid but save it. Add some to the batter if the batter is too dry.

3. Preheat the oven to 350 degrees.

4. Coat of Bundt pan with non-stick spray.

5. Combine the spices and baking soda.

6. Beat the egg, sugar and soaked fruit until they are combined.

7. Add the flour and stir.

8. Add a bit of the tea if the batter is too dry.

9. Transfer the batter to the Bundt pan.

10. Bake for 1 hour.

11. Add your chosen surprise items by pressing them into the cake bottom.

Brownies with Guinness

Cooking Time: 35 minutes

Servings: 6

Ingredients

- 1 cup chocolate stout beer
- 1 ¾ cups shaved semi-sweet chocolate
- ¾ cup butter
- ¾ cup white sugar
- 4 eggs
- 1 cup sugar
- ½ cup chopped walnuts

Icing:

- ¼ cup butter
- 1 cup confectioners' sugar
- 3 tbsp. Irish Cream

Directions:

Preheat the oven to 350 degrees.

Bring the stout to a boil in a pan and set aside

Melt the chocolate using a double boiler. Remove from the stove.

Whip the sugar and eggs with a hand mixer.

Stir in the chocolate and walnuts and combine.

Pour in the beer and stir.

Place the batter in a baking dish.

Bake for 30 minutes.

Let the brownies cool.

While the brownies are baking, whisk the butter and confectioners' sugar together.

Stir in the Irish Cream.

Spread the icing on top of the brownies.

Potato Candy

These aren't potatoes, but they do look like cute little spuds.

Cooking Time: 0

Servings: 60

Ingredients:

- ½ cup butter
- 1 cup cream cheese
- 1 tbsp. vanilla extract
- 1 tbsp. Irish whiskey

- 5 cups confectioners' sugar
- 5 cups coconut flakes
- 3 tbsp. cinnamon
- 3 tbsp. cocoa powder
- ¼ cup almond slivers

Directions:

1. Whip the butter and cream smooth with a hand mixer.

2. Add the vanilla, whiskey and sugar and continue mixing.

3. Integrate the coconut flakes into the mixture.

4. Create little potato-shaped balls.

5. Combine the cinnamon and cocoa powder.

6. Roll the candy in the cinnamon/cocoa mixture.

7. Create "potato eyes" by pressing two almond slivers into the candy.

Creme Brule

A great Irish twist on a wonderful French dessert.

Cooking Time: 1 hour

Servings: 6

Ingredients:

- 2 cups heavy cream
- 1/3 cup white sugar
- 5 egg yolks
- 1 tsp. almond extract

- 3 tbsp. Irish cream liqueur
- ¼ cup heavy cream
- 1 cup whipping cream
- 1 tsp. Irish cream liqueur

Directions:

1. Preheat the oven to 300 degrees.

2. Heat the heavy cream and sugar in a pan and stir until the sugar in dissolved.

3. Whisk the egg yolks, almond extract, and 3 tbsp. liqueur in a bowl.

4. Add 1/3 of the heavy cream, stir, then add the rest and combine. Keep stirring to prevent the yolks from curdling.

5. Transfer the mixture into 6 ramekins.

6. Place the ramekins on a roasting pan.

7. Pour enough boiling water into the pan to cover the ramekins halfway.

8. Bake for 1 hour.

9. While the Brule is cooking, combine the whipping cream with a tbsp. of Irish cream liqueur.

10. Top each cream Brule with a dollop of flavored whipped cream.

Hot Cross Buns

An Easter morning tradition.

Cooking Time: 20 minutes

Servings: 6

Ingredients:

- 1 cup warm skim milk
- ¼ cup butter
- ¼ white sugar
- ¼ tsp. salt

- ½ tsp. cinnamon
- ½ tsp. nutmeg
- ¼ tsp. cloves
- 2 eggs
- 3 cups white flour
- 1 tbsp. active dry yeast
- 1 cup raisins

Icing

- ½ cup confectioners' sugar
- ¼ tsp. vanilla
- 2 tsp. milk

Directions:

1. Combine the skim milk sugar, salt, eggs, spices and yeast in your bread maker.

2. Begin the dough cycle.

3. Five minutes before the end of the knead cycle, add the raisins.

4. Allow the dough to double.

5. Place the dough on a floured surface and punch.

6. Let sit for 15 minutes.

7. Create 15 balls.

8. Place the balls on a coated 9 x 12 baking pan.

9. Cover the baking pan with a damp cloth and let sit for 40 minutes.

10. Bake at 375 degrees for 20 minutes.

11. Slice into 6 separate buns

12. Combine the confectioner's sugar, vanilla and milk with enough water to create a paste.

13. Place the icing in a piping bag and make a crisscross design over each cooled bun.

.

Printed in Great Britain
by Amazon